Grampy N' Leo's Special Day!

Written by Susan Morris
Illustrated by Brooke Sperry

STOP
DO NOT
ENTER

To Jerry and Leo
Love is Forever

Every Thursday morning,
Leo arrives at Grampy's house.

Vroom!

Like a rocket, Leo bursts through the front door,
ready for the day's adventure.

Once, Leo and Grampy watched airplanes take off and land. Another time, they went to the library for story time.

Today, Grampy has something **extra-special** planned. He is taking Leo somewhere new.

ICE CREAM

"Ice cream!" Leo shouts,
looking over all the flavors.
There are so many to choose from.
"Mint chip," Leo declares.

"No, cookies and cream.
Chocolate. Vanilla. Cookie dough."
Grampy grins. "I have an idea."

At the park, Grampy
and Leo find a bench.
Leo savors each lick as it
dribbles down his chin.

PLOP!

Leo wants to speak, but he has no words.

"It's okay, Leo," Grampy promises.

"We'll get you another one."

Leo wants to speak, but he has no words.

"It's okay, Leo," Grampy promises.

"We'll get you another one."

But it is not okay.

Not okay at all.

Today's adventure was no fun.

Leo drags his feet and kicks
the pebbles on the sidewalk.
Grampy wishes he could make
Leo feel better.
But he doesn't know how.

ICE CREAM

Do you want to feed the ducks?"

"NO"

"Do you want to go to the library"?

"NO"

"Do you want to-"

Suddenly, Leo stops.
A grin spreads across his face.

"Grampy, LOOK!"

Grampy takes Leo's hand,
and with an extra bounce in both their steps,
they walk toward MOUNDS AND MOUNDS OF DIRT.

The man driving the dump truck
sees Leo and waves to Leo.
Leo waves back, grinning.
"Want to climb in?" the man asks.

One by one, the men at
the site greet Leo and Grampy.
One by one, they invite him to join them.

MEEP!
MEEP!

On their way home,
Leo swings from Grampy's hand.
"That was so fun!"

"My favorite truck was the bulldozer,"
Grampy says.
"My favorite was the dump truck,"
Leo says. "But I really liked them all."

"I love you, Grampy!"
"I love you too, Leo!"
"Grampy?" Leo says excitedly.
"Yes, Leo?"
"I can't wait to see what you come up with next week!"

Milton Keynes UK
Ingram Content Group UK Ltd.
UKHW051151070524
442334UK00003B/12

9 798218 422004